MY FRIEND
is
Deaf

BY ANNA LEVENE

Chrysalis Education

Distributed in the United States by
Smart Apple Media
1980 Lookout Drive
North Mankato, MN 56003

Copyright © Chrysalis Books PLC 2003

ISBN 1-93233-327-4
Library of Congress Control Number 2003102564

Editorial Manager: Joyce Bentley
Senior Editor: Sarah Nunn
Project Editor: Sue Nicholson
Designer: Wladek Szechter
Photographer: Michael Wicks
Picture Researcher: Terry Forshaw
Illustrations: Tom Connell

Consultant: The National Deaf Children's Society (NDCS)
The National Deaf Children's Society is a U.K. organisation of parents, families, and carers which exists to enable deaf children and young people to maximize their skills and abilities.

The photographer and publishers would like to thank Eva, Sefano and Sophie Stavrou; Majorie Salter; Wladek Szechter; Ruhe; Joe McHale; Bianca; Zeta Jones; and Sue Sharp at the Blanche Neville School for Deaf Children for their help in preparing this book.

Picture acknowledgements:
9 (top), James King-Holmes/Science Photo Library; 10, Royalty-Free/Corbis; 11, Jonathan Blair/Corbis; 13, Adam Woolfitt/Corbis; 15 (top right), Jane Shemilt/Science Photo Library; 15 (bottom) John Birdsall; 19 (bottom), Tyler Gourley/Getty images; 21 (bottom) John Birdsall; 29 (left), Rex Features; 29 (right) John Birdsall

Printed in Hong Kong

10 9 8 7 6 5 4 3 2 1

Contents

*Words in **bold** are explained in the glossary on page 30.*

My friend Daniel

Hi! I'm Amy and this is my friend Daniel. We're both ten years old. We've been good friends for a couple of years now. Before then, I lived with my mom and dad in a different town. Daniel was really nice to me when I first started school here.

Daniel and I live near the park. Last summer we spent a lot of time skateboarding. Daniel's much better than me. I've been a bit nervous ever since I fell off my skateboard and cut my knee really badly. I was with Daniel when it happened. He was ahead of me, and although I shouted he didn't turn round. Daniel hadn't heard me because he's deaf. It took him several minutes to realize I wasn't with him. Then he rushed back to help.

Daniel and Amy love playing in the park near where they live.

Opposite: **This is Daniel. He is ten years old and has been deaf since birth.**

DEAFNESS FACTS

CHILDREN WITH DEAFNESS

In the United States, there are about 28 million people who are deaf or hard of hearing, including 50,000 children who are moderately to profoundly deaf. Many more children have mild deafness, or are deaf in one ear only. Thousands more experience temporary deafness because they have **otitis media**, sometimes called "glue ear," in one or both ears. Most of these children go to ordinary schools and mix with hearing people.

Kinds of deafness

Before I met Daniel, I thought deaf people couldn't hear anything. But now I know that it is rare for someone not to be able to hear any sounds at all. Daniel told me he is moderately to severely deaf. This means that even if we're in a quiet place, he cannot hear what I'm saying without his **hearing aids**. He usually switches them on so that he doesn't have to **lipread** so much.

It's more difficult for Daniel when he's with a group of friends. His hearing aids pick up all sorts of background noises and this makes it hard for him to hear what someone is saying. Daniel can lipread quite well, but not for very long because it's tiring.

If people start talking at the same time, Daniel finds it hard to hear what they are saying.

Opposite: **Amy and Daniel enjoy playing quiet games together. If there is no background noise, Daniel can easily hear everything that Amy says.**

DEAFNESS FACTS

TYPES OF DEAFNESS

Not all deaf people have the same deafness. There are four main types of deafness. This is how people are affected by each type:

Mild: May find it hard to follow speech in a noisy place. If in a quiet place, may not have any difficulty talking to one person. Unlikely to wear hearing aids.

Moderate: Need to wear hearing aids. Find it very difficult to hear in a noisy place. Will lipread.

Severe: Need hearing aids, find lipreading important, and may use **sign language** as well as speaking.

Profound: Find lipreading very important and may prefer using sign language instead of speaking. Hearing aids may not help.

Deaf from birth

Daniel told me he was born deaf, although nobody knew about his deafness until he was one. Before then, he seemed just like any other baby. Daniel's mom likes showing me pictures of him when he was little. Daniel thinks they're boring!

Both Daniel's parents can hear, so they thought Daniel could, too. But when he was eight months old his mum took him for a hearing check. The health visitor shook a rattle behind Daniel's head, but Daniel didn't look round to see where the sound was coming from. The health visitor said Daniel should have some more hearing tests at hospital.

So Daniel was given different kinds of hearing tests. Then, just after his first birthday, Daniel's parents were told that he was deaf in both ears.

This baby is having a special hearing test to check that its inner ears are working properly.

Opposite: Daniel's mom likes showing Amy pictures of Daniel as a baby. Daniel was just over a year old before doctors were certain that he was deaf.

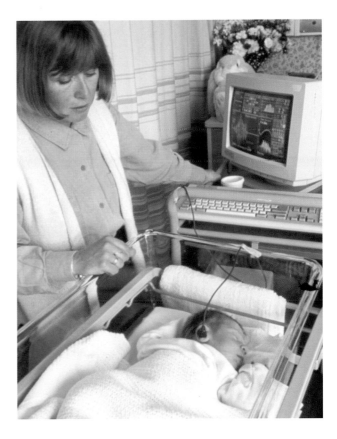

DEAFNESS FACTS

WHY ARE SOME BABIES BORN DEAF?

Some children are born deaf for no obvious reason. Others become deaf because they were born early or because of a shortage of oxygen in their blood during birth. Sometimes deafness can be passed down in families. It can also be caused by an infectious disease, such as measles, mumps, or meningitis. All babies are now to be checked for deafness shortly after birth, so they can be given the help they need as soon as possible.

Over 90 percent of deaf babies are born into families with no history of deafness.

What is sound?

I sometimes wonder what it must be like to hear as little as Daniel. There are so many different sounds! I love the sound of water trickling over pebbles, or my feet swishing through fall leaves. Our teacher, Miss Nelson, told us the loudness of a sound is measured in **decibels**.

She explained that all sounds are made up of vibrations rippling through the air. The ripples are called sound waves. Waves that follow each other very quickly produce higher-pitched sounds, while slower-moving waves produce lower-pitched sounds. This is why high sounds are called high **frequency**, and low sounds are called low frequency.

Frequency is measured in **Hertz**.

A barking dog is about 500 Hertz; a helicopter is about 4,000 Hertz.

A dog's bark measures around 500 Hertz.

DEAFNESS FACTS

FREQUENCY, OR PITCH

Speech is a mix of high and low frequency sounds. Letters such as p, g, and k are a higher frequency than vowels such as o, a, and e. Someone who is deaf may easily mix up sounds at a similar frequency. For example, they might hear the word "pick" as "kick", or "mean" as "bean"—so a sentence like "pick your own beans" could end up sounding very odd!

The loudness of a sound is measured in decibels.

150 Rocket take-off

140 Pain threshold

130 Jet aircraft taking off

110 Thunder

100 Pneumatic drill

This worker is wearing earmuffs to protect his ears while he is using a noisy pneumatic drill.

90 Heavy traffic

70 Orchestra

50 Normal conversation

30 Whispering

20 Falling leaves

10 Hearing threshold (the level at which sound can be heard)

Inside the ear

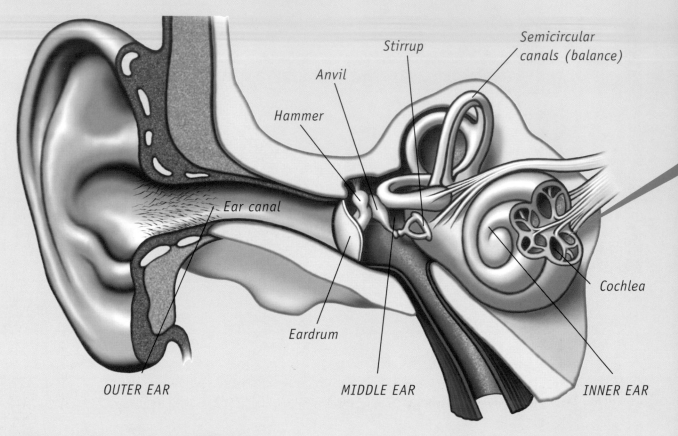

Stirrup

Semicircular
canals (balance)

Anvil

Hammer

Ear canal

Cochlea

Eardrum

OUTER EAR

MIDDLE EAR

INNER EAR

HOW THE EAR WORKS

Most of your ears are inside your head. The outer parts that you can see are there to funnel sound waves into your ear canals and eardrums.

Your eardrum is a thin piece of skin stretched across the end of your ear canal. When sound waves touch the eardrum, it vibrates. The vibrations then pass from the eardrum through three small bones called the hammer, the anvil, and the stirrup to a coiled tube called the **cochlea**. Inside the cochlea are thousands of tiny hair cells. As sound vibrations reach the hair cells, the hairs move and change the vibrations into electrical signals. These signals travel along the auditory nerve to the brain. The brain then decodes them and you hear. Daniel is deaf because his cochlea cannot change sound vibrations into electrical signals. This kind of deafness is called sensori-neural deafness.

Close-up of tiny hair cells in the cochlea

Movement of the hair cells in the cochlea are converted into electrical signals. These travel along nerves to your brain where they are given meaning.

Right: A whirling fairground ride can make you feel sick and dizzy. This is because your brain cannot process quickly enough all the messages it receives from your ears.

Your ears have another important job—they help you keep your balance. When you move your head, liquid inside your ears' semicircular canals pushes against hair-like nerve endings. The nerve endings send messages to your brain. Your brain then works out what position your head is in. If your head is moving very fast, your brain can't process the messages quickly enough, and you may feel sick or dizzy.

Hearing aids

Outside, or in noisy places, Daniel turns down the volume on his hearing aids.

Most of the time Daniel wears hearing aids. He wears one behind each ear. They each have a tiny **microphone** inside, which picks up sounds and makes them louder. Daniel can turn the volume up or down.

Daniel says his hearing aids have been specially tuned to suit his level of deafness. They give exactly the right boost to the sound waves that reach his inner ear. Every few months Daniel goes for a check-up to see if his hearing has changed. If it has, his hearing aids must be re-tuned.

Daniel's hearing aids are connected to plastic molds. The molds have been made specially to fit snugly inside his ears. Two or three times a year Daniel has to have new molds fitted because he has grown out of the old ones.

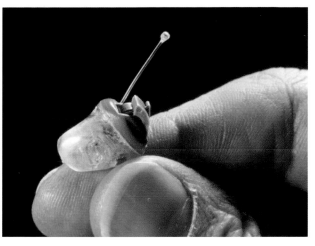

In-the-ear hearing aid

Like most deaf children, Daniel wears behind-the-ear hearing aids.

DEAFNESS FACTS

TYPES OF HEARING AID

Daniel's hearing aids are called behind-the-ear aids. Most children wear this type of hearing aid so that when their ear molds need changing, the whole hearing aid does not have to be changed, too. Other types include in-the-ear (ITE) aids, and in-the-canal (ITC) aids. These are usually worn by people with mild to moderate deafness.

COCHLEAR IMPLANTS

Some children or adults with severe or profound deafness are fitted with **cochlear implants**, which are placed inside the cochlea in the inner ear. Instead of magnifying sounds, the implants send electrical signals directly to the brain.

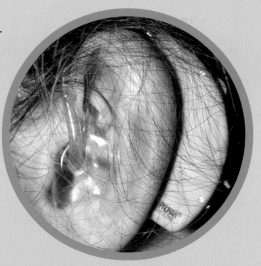

Behind-the-ear hearing aid

At school

Daniel always wears his hearing aids at school and usually sits near the front of the class. In lessons he uses a **radio aid** so that he doesn't miss anything Miss Nelson says. She wears a microphone around her neck, which directs her voice straight into Daniel's hearing aids. Even when she turns her back, he can still hear what she is saying.

At break-time, people play noisy games and shout a lot. Daniel often finds it hard to hear what's being said. He hates it when he misses a joke. By the time I've told him the punch line, everyone else has stopped laughing and I know he feels very left out.

Daniel often has problems understanding what's being said in sports classes, too. Our gym is so big and echoing that you can't hear anything clearly. Miss Nelson has to make sure Daniel's next to her when she tells the class what to do or he won't understand.

Above: **Daniel finds it difficult to hear in large echoing spaces, such as gyms and sports halls.**

Left: **Daniel enjoys working on computers because he does not need to worry too much about hearing sounds.**

Opposite: **Daniel's teacher wears a special radio aid around her neck. The radio aid transmits her voice straight into Daniel's hearing aids.**

DEAFNESS FACTS

RADIO AIDS

There is a lot of background noise in a classroom and this makes it hard to hear what the teacher is saying. Radio aids help because they send sound directly from the teacher to the pupil. Radio aids have two parts. The teacher wears a radio transmitter and microphone. The child wears a radio receiver, which picks up the sounds from the teacher's transmitter.

Visiting Amy's grandma

On the way home, Daniel and I sometimes visit my grandma. My grandma's quite old and her hearing isn't very good. We usually have to knock really loudly on the door or shout through the letterbox.

My grandma started going deaf a few years ago. When she was

younger, she worked in a noisy factory. In those days, nobody wore ear protectors because people didn't realize that loud sounds could damage your hearing. Now she's always saying to me, "Remember not to play your music too loud, young lady!"

From time to time, my grandma gets a whistling noise in her ears called tinnitus. Even when she's wearing her hearing aid, the tinnitus makes it hard for her to chat. Sometimes, it even stops her sleeping.

Opposite: **Amy's grandma is going deaf. She often doesn't hear the doorbell, so Amy shouts through the letterbox.**

Most older people have some deafness. Some wear hearing aids, but many don't want to admit that they cannot hear as well as they used to.

DEAFNESS FACTS

OTITIS MEDIA ("GLUE EAR")

Both Daniel and Amy's grandma have forms of permanent deafness. But most deafness is not permanent. Some children can't hear properly because they have a sticky fluid in their middle ear, which can cause **conductive deafness**. Otitis media (which some people call "glue ear") often clears up by itself but sometimes an operation is needed to drain away the fluid. This is done by placing tiny tubes, called **grommets**, inside the ear.

When swimming, children with grommets often wear swimming plugs in their ears so that they don't get an ear infection from the water.

At Daniel's house

Textphones make it easier for deaf people to communicate with other people.

I love going to Daniel's because he has some really cool machines. His dad has just bought a textphone. When Daniel wants to call a friend, he simply types in what he wants to say. Daniel also has his own computer so he can send emails or talk on the internet.

For his birthday, Daniel got a cell phone so now he can text his friends. We spend a lot of time talking to each other on our phones. We use them to fix times and places to meet, or just to talk.

If we watch television, Daniel sometimes finds it difficult to follow the story. There might be several people talking at once, or you may not be able to see the face of the person who's speaking—so we usually go and do something else. If it's a really good program, Daniel can use a special pair of headphones that make it easier for him to understand what's being said. He doesn't like using them, though. He says they make him feel cut off from everyone else in the room.

Cell phones are a great way for deaf people to talk to their friends.

DEAFNESS FACTS

GADGETS

Nowadays, there are all sorts of gadgets that deaf people can use in their homes. For example, lights can be wired to flash when the doorbell or phone rings or if a smoke alarm goes off. There are also alarm clocks that vibrate or turn on a light when it's time to get up.

A vibrating alarm clock is put under a pillow.

Using sign language

Many deaf children go to deaf clubs where they can talk to friends using sign language.

Both Daniel's parents are hearing, so most of the time they speak to him just like they do to me. But they also talk to him in sign language with their hands. Each sign means a different word. When Daniel was little, his mom or dad used to sign a word and say it at the same time. Daniel watched their lips and learned to copy the shapes their lips made. This helped him to speak clearly.

Daniel also uses sign language to communicate with other deaf children. Once a month, he and his mom and dad go to a club for deaf children and their parents. Daniel likes meeting other deaf children. He says it's easier to feel part of a gang there. A few months ago, Daniel introduced me to some of his friends from the club. For a joke, they had a long talk in sign language. I felt really left out. Now I know what it's like for Daniel when we're all talking and laughing and he can't hear what's being said.

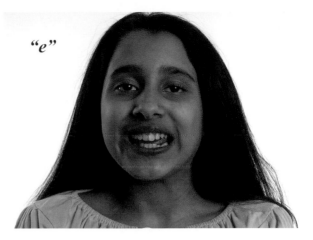

"e"

"A" American fingerspelling

"A" British fingerspelling

"o"

DEAFNESS FACTS

SIGN LANGUAGE

In North America, many deaf people use American Sign Language (ASL), which uses signs for whole words and ideas. There is not one world sign language. Each country has its own. At least 500,000 people in the U.S. and Canada use ASL and it is taught in many schools and colleges.

Fingerspelling is used to sign names and places or a word that doesn't have a special sign of its own.

"th"

Try copying these mouth shapes and see what sounds you make. Now ask a few friends to cover their ears and guess what sounds you are making. Are they right?

At the clinic

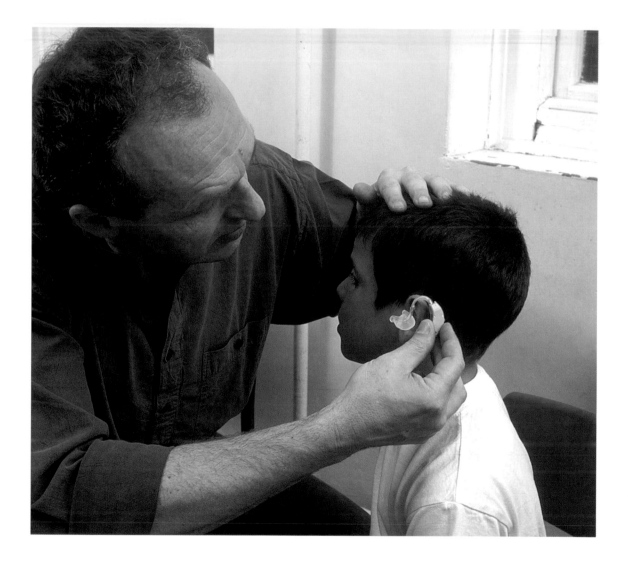

While Daniel is still growing quickly, he goes to the clinic every two or three months to have his hearing aids checked. Daniel says,

"If my aids don't fit well, I can't hear properly. What's worse, they start making a whistling sound, which gets really annoying!

"If I need new molds, Doctor Hunt squirts a kind of putty into my ears. This tells him what shape and size the new molds need to be. The putty molds are sent off to a workshop, which uses them to make the plastic molds.

"Sometimes I also have my hearing checked to see if it has changed. Doctor Hunt gives me special headphones to wear, then asks me to press a button when I hear a click. This makes a light come up on Doctor Hunt's machine. He makes sure I can't see him operating the machine! The results are shown on a kind of chart called an **audiogram**. Doctor Hunt compares this audiogram with previous audiograms. So far, my hearing has stayed the same."

Opposite: ***Daniel's hearing aids are checked every few months to make sure that they fit properly.***

Doctor Hunt shows Daniel and his mom the results of Daniel's hearing tests.

DEAFNESS FACTS

PROGRESSIVE DEAFNESS

As children grow, their hearing can change, so their hearing aids must be re-tuned. Some children have **progressive deafness**, which means that their hearing gets worse as they get older. These children need to know how fast their hearing is getting worse so that they and their families can plan ahead. For example, they may want to learn to sign, or find out about schools for the deaf.

At Amy's house

At weekends, Daniel sometimes spends the night at my house. When he first came, my parents thought they had to speak very loudly so he could understand them. Daniel looked a bit scared. When I asked him what was wrong, he said he didn't like people shouting because it made them look angry. Also, it was harder for him to lipread because their lips made different shapes from usual. My mom and dad were really embarrassed!

Now everyone speaks normally to Daniel. In fact, my family is so used to him they sometimes forget he can't hear as well as us. My little sister is the worst. Even when she's eating she talks so fast that Daniel can't follow her at all.

"Slow down!" he once begged. "Please don't talk with your mouth full. And could you look at me when you speak? Otherwise I don't know if you're saying something to me, to that pigeon outside or even to the Man on the Moon!"

"Sorry Daniel," she said and we all laughed.

It's hard to lipread when someone is eating!

Opposite: **Daniel watches Amy's lips when she speaks to help him understand what she's saying.**

DEAFNESS FACTS

LIP READING

Deaf people watch how people's lips form different shapes as they speak. They then work out which patterns of shapes belong to different words. Short words, such as "I" or "me" are obviously easier to work out than longer words. Ask a friend to say a long word to you (such as "telephone") silently, without telling you what it is. Can you work out what is being said?

Questions people ask

Q. **What's the best way to speak to a deaf person?**

A. Make sure you have their attention before you start talking.

- Keep good eye contact and speak clearly but naturally.
- Do not speak too quickly or too slowly or you will make it harder for them to lipread.
- Pause between sentences and make sure that they have understood what you are saying.
- If they do not understand a word or phrase, try a different one.
- If you are in a group, try to make sure only one person speaks at a time.
- If you are inside, go into a room with curtains and a carpet—your voice will not echo as much.
- Switch off the television, radio, or music center—deaf people find it hard to hear if there is background noise.
- Do not eat, chew gum, or cover your mouth while you are speaking.
- Try to make sure your face is well lit.

Q. **How long does it take to learn how to sign?**

A. If a child starts learning to sign when he or she is very young and has lots of help from parents and school, it will usually take no longer to learn to sign than it took you to learn to speak. If he or she starts later, and the parents are also learning, it can take much longer.

Q. **Are there any jobs deaf people cannot do?**

A. Only a very few. As equipment has improved, more and more deaf people have been able to work in all kinds of places. They are also helped by new technology, such as computers and the internet, through which it is possible to communicate by email rather than by speaking on the telephone.

Q. **Can deaf people play music?**

A. Yes. Even profoundly deaf people are sensitive to vibrations and can feel them as sound. One of the best-known percussionists in the world, Evelyn Glennie, is profoundly deaf.

Q. **Will listening to loud music make me deaf?**

A. If you listen to very loud music over a number of years, the tiny hair cells inside your cochlea will die and your hearing will be permanently damaged. Many older rock and pop musicians suffer some kind of deafness.

Virtual sign language computer software is being developed that will help deaf people in their everyday lives.

Q. **Are there any other aids to help deaf people?**

A. Yes, just as some blind people have guide dogs to help them around, some deaf people have "hearing" dogs to alert them to everyday sounds in their homes, such as the ringing of the doorbell. **Subtitles** on television screens can help people understand what is happening in a program or on the news. In the future, many homes may have a **videophone** so that deaf people can communicate by lipreading and sign language. There is also computer software that translates spoken words into sign language.

Q. **Could you hear without ears?**

A. You could hear without outer ears (the bits you can see), but not as clearly because the outer ears act as funnels to channel sound to the inner ears (the parts of your ears inside your head).

Q. **How do animals hear?**

A. All vertebrates (animals with backbones) have the same sort of middle-ear structure as humans, but not all have eardrums. For example, fish and some species of snake do not have external ears. Instead, they receive sound waves through their bodies, through the water, or the ground. Bats have huge external ears for their size. As they fly, they make high-pitched squeaks which bounce off nearby objects as echoes. From the strength and direction of the echoes, the bats can work out where the objects are.

Subtitles can help deaf people follow television programs.

Glossary

audiogram This charts a person's hearing levels. It shows whether a person has normal hearing or some degree of deafness. It also shows the level of deafness and which frequencies are affected.

cochlea Part of the inner ear which helps us hear by converting the loudness and frequency of sounds into electrical signals that are sent to the brain.

cochlear implant A type of tiny hearing aid put inside the cochlea in the inner ear to help people with severe or profound deafness. Instead of magnifying sounds, the implant sends electrical signals directly to the brain.

conductive deafness A type of deafness that affects the outer or middle ears, not the inner ear, and is the most common form of deafness. Conductive deafness can often be treated but some forms are permanent.

decibel A unit used to measure the loudness of sound. Normal conversation is around 50 decibels. An orchestra playing is around 70 decibels. People who are exposed to over 80 decibels of sound regularly and for long periods of time may permanently damage their hearing.

fingerspelling A kind of language using hands and fingers in which each letter of the alphabet has its own sign. In Great Britain, finger- spelling uses two hands. In America, it uses one hand.

frequency (or pitch) How low or how high a sound is, measured in Hertz.

grommets Small plastic tubes put into the eardrum to stop more sticky fluid building up inside the middle ear. Grommets usually fall out by themselves. Occasionally, they need to be removed.

hearing aids Devices that make sounds louder. A hearing aid may be worn behind the ear or in the ear.

Hertz Measurement of sound vibrations per second. Humans can only hear sounds measuring between about 130 and 600 Hertz. Animals such as bats or dogs can hear sounds at a much higher frequency.

lipread To work out what someone is saying by trying to "read" the shape of their lips as they talk.

microphone A device that picks up sound waves.

otitis media Thick, sticky fluid in the middle ear that causes temporary deafness.

progressive deafness When someone's hearing gets steadily worse as they get older.

radio aid A device which sends radio waves from one person to another. The radio waves are converted into sound waves and made louder through a hearing aid or radio receiver.

sign language A way of communicating using the hands and body language, in which signs stand for whole words and ideas. Different countries have their own sign languages.

subtitles Words appearing on television screens to help people who cannot hear well understand what is happening in a program.

videophones Telephones that allow you to see, as well as talk to, the person at the other end.

Useful organizations

HERE ARE SOME ORGANIZATIONS YOU MIGHT LIKE TO CONTACT FOR MORE INFORMATION ABOUT DEAFNESS

NATIONAL ASSOCIATION FOR THE DEAF

814 Thayer Ave, Suite 250,
Silver Spring, MD 20910-4500
www.nad.org
Email: nadinfo@nad.org
Safeguards rights and supports America's 28 million people who are deaf or hard of hearing.

ALEXANDER GRAHAM BELL ASSOCIATION FOR THE DEAF

3417 Volta Place, NW,
Washington DC, 20007
Tel: 202-337-5220
Provides information on hearing loss and will answer questions. Summer camps for children who are deaf or hard of hearing are listed on:
www.agbell.org/information/camps.htm

AMERICAN SOCIETY FOR DEAF CHILDREN

PO Box 3355,
Gettysburg, PA 17325
Email: ASDCL@aol.org
www.deafchildren.org
Gives information to families with children who are deaf or hard of hearing. Non-profit parent-to-parent support.

NATIONAL INFORMATION CENTER FOR CHILDREN AND YOUTHS WITH DISABILITIES

PO Box 1492,
Washington DC 20013-1492
www.nichcy.org
Supplies fact sheets, publications, and other information.

OTHER WEBSITES

www.childrenwithdisabilities.nejrs.org
Supplies information and links to other sites.

Index